QUIET
OWLS

by Joelle Riley

PULL AHEAD BOOKS

Animals

Lerner Publications Company • Minneapolis

This book is available in two editions:
Library binding by Lerner Publications Company, a division of Lerner Publishing Group, Inc.
Soft cover by First Avenue Editions, an imprint of Lerner Publishing Group, Inc.
241 First Avenue North
Minneapolis, MN 55401 U.S.A.

Website address: www.lernerbooks.com

Words in *italic* type are explained in a glossary on page 30.

Library of Congress Cataloging-in-Publication Data

Riley, Joelle.
    Quiet owls / by Joelle Riley.
        p.   cm. — (Pull ahead books)
    Summary: Simple text describes the physical characteristics, habitat, life cycle, and behavior of the owl, including how this quiet hunter finds prey.
    ISBN-13: 978–0–8225–3771–7 (lib. bdg. : alk. paper)
    ISBN-10: 0–8225–3771–0 (lib. bdg. : alk. paper)
    ISBN-13: 978–0–8225–9889–3 (pbk. : alk. paper)
    ISBN-10: 0–8225–9889–2 (pbk. : alk. paper)
    1. Owls—Juvenile literature. [1. Owls.] I. Title.
II. Series.
QL696.S83R55 2004
598.9'7—dc22   2003012847

Manufactured in the United States of America
2 3 4 5 6 7 — JR — 12 11 10 09 08 07

A bird is sitting in this tree.

What kind of bird is it?

This bird is
an owl.
Some owls
are small.

Other owls
are big.
Where do
owls live?

Many owls live in forests.

Some owls live in cold places,
where few trees grow.

Owls have big heads
and round faces.

They see and hear well.

An owl's body is covered
with soft feathers.

Why do owls
need soft
feathers?

Soft feathers help owls to fly quietly.

Owls are so quiet that
they can surprise other animals.

Owls are *predators.*
They hunt and eat other animals.

Owls hunt and eat animals such as rabbits, birds, and mice.

The animals an owl hunts
are called its *prey*.

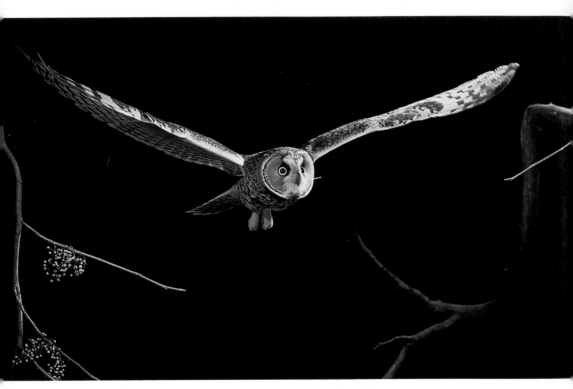

An owl watches and listens for prey.
Then the owl tries to catch the prey.

This quiet owl is swooping down.
The mouse does not hear the owl.

Quick as a
flash, the
owl grabs
the mouse.

An owl has sharp claws on its feet.
The claws are called *talons.*

An owl's talons hold prey tightly.

An owl takes its prey to a safe place and eats it.

The owl eats even tough parts, such as bones and fur.

The owl's stomach makes the
tough bits into a neat little bundle.

The bundle is called a *pellet*.
The owl spits out the pellet.

You might find pellets
near an owl's nest.

Owls' nests are in trees,
on cliffs, or on the ground.

An owl has laid three eggs in this nest.

Baby owls will hatch from the eggs.

Owls sit on their eggs
to keep them warm.

If eggs get cold,
the babies won't hatch.

Look! Two baby owls have hatched.

A baby owl is called an *owlet*.

Owlets are covered with fuzzy feathers called *down.*

Owlets grow fast.
They need to eat lots of food.

These owlets are very hungry.
How will they get food?

The owlets' parents hunt for prey.
The parents bring food to the nest.

The owlets gobble up every bit.

Owlets grow and grow.
Their feathers begin to change.

Instead of down, the owlets grow
long, soft feathers.

The owlets climb around
outside the nest.

They practice flapping their wings.
They grow stronger each day.

The young owls learn how to fly
and how to hunt for prey.

They have become quiet hunters.

KEY:

▨ shows where owls live

Find your state or province on this map.
Do quiet owls live near you?

Parts of an Owl's Body

head

eye

wing

beak

feathers

tail

leg

foot

talon

Glossary

down: short, fuzzy feathers

owlet: a baby owl

pellet: a small bundle that an owl spits out after it eats an animal. The pellet contains the tough bits of the animal's body, such as bones, fur, or feathers.

predators: animals that hunt and eat other animals

prey: the animals an owl hunts

talons: an owl's sharp claws

Hunt and Find

About the Author

Joelle Riley grew up in Pennsylvania. Once she went with her class on a field trip to the National Museum of Natural History in Washington, D.C. An exhibit about the then-endangered peregrine falcon got her interested in owls and other birds of prey. Now she lives in Minnesota with two cats and two greyhounds. She likes to walk her dogs along the Mississippi River and watch for signs of owls and other wildlife.

Photo Acknowledgments

The photographs in this book are reproduced with the permission of: © Charles Melton/Visuals Unlimited, p. 3; © Todd Fink/Daybreak Imagery, pp. 4, 23; © P. Lindholm/Visuals Unlimited, p. 5; © Gerard Fuehrer/ Visuals Unlimited, p. 6; © Joe McDonald/Visuals Unlimited, pp. 7, 8, 10, 12, 13, 27; © Jim Yokajty/The Image Finders, p. 9; © Richard Day/ Daybreak Imagery, pp. 11, 17, 21, 25, 26; © Warren Williams/ Visuals Unlimited, p. 14; © Arthur Morris/Visuals Unlimited, p. 15; © Robert Clay/ Visuals Unlimited, p. 16; © John D. Cunningham/Visuals Unlimited, p. 18; © Rick & Nora Bowers/Visuals Unlimited, pp. 19, 31; © Michael S. Quinton/Visuals Unlimited, p. 20; © Maslowski/ Visuals Unlimited, pp. 22, 24.

The cover image appears courtesy of © Richard Day/Daybreak Imagery.